More than a man in a boat

Michael Baron

© Michael Baron 2010
Published by Octogenary Press, Cockermouth
ISBN: 978-0-9565134-0-3
All rights reserved
Designed by Smith+Bell Design (www.smithplusbell.com)
Cover illustration by Hellie Mulvaney
Printed by Russell Press (www.russellpress.com)

For Hetty, Timothy, Joanna, Saskia,
Jacob, Hellie, Phoebe and Jan

Acknowledgments

Thanks to the editors of the following for publishing some of the poems in this collection – *The Jewish Quarterly, Jewish Renaissance, Other Poetry, Pitch, Ploughshare, On A Bat's Wing,* and *World Haiku Review.* Also BBC Radio Merseyside, Radio Cumbria, www.wah.org.uk, www.write-away-poetry.org and www.poetrybay.com. And thanks for the support of the poets of Cumbrian Poets Workshop, the late William Scammell, and the encouragement of Arvon (paid for by a generous Cumbria County Council) and Ty Newydd, and their tutors, Michael Longley, Piotr Sommer and Gillian Clarke. And not to forget the designers, Andy Smith and Denise Bell, Joanna Baron who laboured over her Mac to put the poems into legible form, Hellie Mulvaney for the original cover, Jeremy and Marita Over, and Stevie Krayer for advice and encouragement.

Contents

Defining Paradise

Wondering about paradise
isn't easy this prelapsarian hour.
Do scrabbling blackbirds in my apple tree notice
the freeze of October grass,
my gaudy fuchsias in terminal undress,
leaves deformed like old mens' fingers?

And if I died now hearing the coal tit
feasting on window putties, would it
be proper with so much autumn welcome
going on with gusto just over there?
Those greylags make a hell of a noise
ploughing up the surface of the lake.
And you, you, sashay into the room
saying with conviction, Jews don't have
paradise... you can't expire here;
you need the Garden.

I'm none too pleased about snakes.
Even if I was on a chaise-longue
and they came petitioners to my washstand,
me in a damp blue nightshirt waiting
in a *small private apartment*, cash ready
for liftman, doctor, undertaker, policeman.
The trouble, my dear, is the lexicon.
The book we can't do without, though
it's true we've managed, penniless
in dusty towns before exchanges opened.

But *le mot juste* we need for water, too.
So get it right, get it right, just this once.
Paradise is *park or pleasure ground.*
a Vauxhall where younger lovers wander,

and fornicate to music of the spheres
played with encores on ancient strings.
And you say that's not for me?
Where should the happy dead go, huh?
Somewhere between the lake's darklined
margin and the shit-spattered shingle,
there's room to slip and slide away?
The text, my dear, the text.
Any place or state of bliss.
Stay with me longer then, stay.
Let the sun burrow out from rockface.
as today with surprise, lighting
this *park in which foreign animals are kept.*
The cows by the gate stamp hooves.
slobber, slowly deflower a birch,
branches thin as childrens' arms.

We'll go through all this tomorrow –
if I am here – and I'll shout, I'll shout,
Paradise... *Gan Eden.**

* *Gan Eden.* Hebrew for the Garden of Eden

Dance Positions

I hold you in the mirror of my arms,
and then, reversing swiftly,
the sun's across your back
lined like reeds in water,
you hold me.

This choreography we practise
is an old event yet we old
practitioners of the art
don't tire.

Each private dance
a first performance,
excites as undiscovered stars
seen through antique telescopes.

Each dance a homage,
each a hidden rite.

What If They Were Larks

yo-yo-ing secretly
over the regimented pines
and if the song was
larksong and there were only
my footfalls and the river song
from the equally secret leaf-filled
valley beneath my feet
and the forest was
open just to us

skylark and man
singing and walking
listening
breathing the green air
would it have been enough?

She Painted The Tree...

She painted the tree
as she had always done
from colour of rainbows,
a branch a hogshair brush,
twigs specks of burnt sienna,
leaves stabs of Hooker's Green
slicked in by a palette knife
sharp as thorns.

Left it to dry, and
closed the door quietly
(the way a lover goes).
Overnight, alone, content,
she dreamt top-soil, compost, mould,
the sexy in-and-out earth worm slither.
Waking, sated, smelt broken clods,
saw curtains open on clays made gold,

turned a key, the door rustling
into a garden and the tree
was heavy with blossom, boughs
bent with it, spread with it
out of windows over the street.
All day people filled baskets of petals,
told their children,
who told their friends.

When night knocked like a shy policeman,
the tree surrendered, defenceless,
exhausted from so much fecundity,
such wild lust to be alive,
became an ordinary lovely thing.
Flat. Another canvas, paint-laden,
hoist to a cheap easel for old voyeurs
to touch, desire, ask *'how much?'*

Anti-Pastorale

December pastorals begin
'*Now the fields are dark with rain...*'
Etc. Continue to explain
in words tired as yesterday
why rooks are flying west
where one star alarms the sky.

December pastorals begin
without a smell of anoraks or boots.
'*Beech trees are naked to their roots...*'
Etc. Forget that crowd of greylags
arguing, wary of walkers' shiny sticks,
and sullen sheep on anorexic grass.

December pastorals begin
high in a study, beneath a lamp,
the screen's blank, software corrupt.
'*Who nailed this badger to the fence...*'
Etc. The felt is flapping in the eaves,
wheelbarrow bust, cold frame smashed.

December pastorals begin
like prompts from women with guitars.
She frets; he'll write poetic lies,
conceits, odd marriages of ideas.
'*Winds are dissonant on winter nights...*'
Etc... Arpeggios linger round the ear.

Royal Marriage

The union was one of monarchs,
kings and queens of afternoons,
comets joined in fiery courses,
glowing, glowing, going, gone.

Later; tears, wet under hand,
her mouth widening,
compelled obeisance,
and, treaty sealed, joy erupts.

Doubtless a thousand limbs
in realms across the earth
moved thus and thus. But this,
this there then now how how.

Oh hold me now and wait,
you warm wise man
why make us so alive?

Us

When they had finished walking,
Holme Wood about them, and closing,
there was no other way to go,
no place with redemption to offer.
The man looked at his son, standing,
tall, round-shouldered, distant,
white water at the beck's edge,
white water thrusting into grey
and black, turning over, over
in somersaults of autumn fury.
Saw the lake capture it, head-on,
and calmed by the wider flood,
sink deep in mirrors of larch.

He had this flat stone in his hand.
plucked from the flood,
yet lacked a name for something
hard, and cold between fingers,
nails bitten to moons of nothing.
One dream exhaled its sigh,
exhausted. Always it died – years,
long days of watching, hours,
so eager for word marvels.
Tell him how was it within
that body, round shoulder,
crooked joint of thumb?

Tensed his feet on the beach,
pike pools emptying, drying out,
as rain washed quickly past
to another valley, beyond the fell.
Began to push boots deep
into a scrum of shingle as if,
as if wishing to disappear, become
stone he could not eat, nor skim,
define its geology, feel, colour,
shape; nor know lake smells.
Words wounded, and lost,
vocabulary blank pages.

Pedlar

No horse or cart. Got rides.
Walked. 400 versts. Slept in barns.
Then stood long days in markets
thickening with noise. Sometimes
in hostile towns placed
his basket lined with linen
on edge of pavements.
Back turned to carriages, slapped
by mud, winced at sting of stones
on the torn gaberdine coat
his wife's uncle loaned him.

Never without a tie, a white tight
collar chafed his chicken neck;
it didn't matter how he looked.
Each waiting Friday he returned,
always coming home at sunset
to empty bags of roubles
on the table, set the candles.
All this he did for her
who saw him as shadow only,

dark shape, dim curve of husband,
could not count the blisters
on dust-dirt feet, worry
over chewed-down finger nails.
At night, gently she traced
journey lines across his face,
teased in bed the muscles
of bony thighs; heard that cough.

All this for her, six children – and
when he died, after the funeral –
the Great Synagogue too big
to silence lamentations –
after prayers and endless sitting,
(the eldest called to serve the Czar),
they left. Journeyed 400 miles.
Took passage, left 400 years.

Five certificates of marriage
(black ink fades quickly)
declared a barely remembered father
Pedlar.
Voted Liberal. Cheered
when Mafeking was relieved.

Walking in Weimar, 2008

A Short and Statuesque History of the Enlightenment Without Name-Dropping

That's him there
and him there
oh and him there
and her
where there him her there
alone together
them everywhere.

Conjunctions
(to Piotr Sommer)

My wife's great-grandmother, Johanna,
selling ribbons on the Frauenplan in Weimar,
saw Goethe leaning at his door.
Perhaps my great-grandfather, Meir,
peddling pans, touched a shiny cap
to yours in Warsawa, Plock, Lodz, Otwock.
and said '*dobry dzien*'.
as I do now.

If

William and Dorothy
had wintered here
instead of Goslar,
walked with Goethe
in the Ducal park,
admired his Garten-haus,
taken tea with Anna Amelia,
viewed her library
splendid in white and gold?

Marktplatz

Beside Hotel Elefant
a wall without a window
Bach *hier gewohnt*
an 'Elektrik' van
parked
on his best clavier.

Road Sign

Cranach-Haus
Schillers-Wohnhaus
Gingko-Museum
Buchenwald-Gedenkstatte

Learning Welsh – 3rd September 1939

(i.m. Richard Jehu Mills)

*'...I have to tell you that no such undertaking has been received
and that consequently this country is at war with Germany.'*
(Neville Chamberlain)

We stood, listening, under a borrowed brolly,
(he in tweed plus-fours, me in shorts)
outside the police-station in Dolgellau.
I never asked my father why he turned
down the invitation to step inside
that warm wet ending afternoon.

I guess he was alone. Somewhere I could
not reach, testing words against eventuality.
What next, how soon, where, what he'd seen
in Berlin two months before, sizing shadows
moving close and closer. Not the rain
coursing raggedly in ditches, the old sun
going. Not the man to hear any bird sing
(or know its name apart from sparrow).

We walked up the lane, hand-in-hand,
(he in tweed plus-fours, me in shorts)
to the green tents on a sloping field.
My brother playing rounders, unconcerned,
with Dafydd, Gwilym, farm boys, and rough;
my sister lost in 'Milly Molly Mandy' games.
Later the elders leaving to sort things out,
tents were taken down, packed away.

Sudden orphans, we ate with Dafydd,
Gwilym, inhabited strange beds, lit candles,
learnt other words, in Welsh – *'cau dy geg'*.*

*Shut up

Memoir Of Uncle M

(from lines suggested by Sean O'Brien)

The unloved upright piano in the Playhouse
sprang a last dark E flat chord and died.
Shutting hard as pain that beer-stained top,
Uncle rose, bowed once to face the crowd –
of three. Aunt Mae (with her valuable violin),
my mother, and in short grey trousers, me.

High in the empty gallery, dim with dust,
he saw his childhood furies, watching,
old Vogel's ghost from the Academy
dovening to his parents dressed for *shabbas*.
He was the family Rubinstein, their hope.
'Our Myer' was engineered for concert halls.

For him, the star – Wigmore, Queens, Carnegie.
They knew applause before they heard 'bravo',
dreamed the smart white tie, tails; signed
programmes at stage doors. Such flowers! Reviews!
Added up the cards on the narrow mantle-piece,
in *shul* nodded like a metronome to every glance.

'*Our Myer*' ran off to sea. Grandpa burnt his music,
sheet by sheet – Chopin, Brahms. Grandma sold
the Broadwood to Mrs Teitlebaum next door.
Her cross-eyed daughter, Sarah, practised scales
at night. Such promise would condemn her
to a life of teaching arpeggios to spotty boys.

'*My heart he broke*' – his father cried to kind enquirers.
Daily, in the parlour of the narrow mantlepiece,
reads aloud the shipping news in the Telegraph.
Climbs forty steps to the attic room in tears,
Cuts cloth, chalks and measures silk lapels.
Jarrow tramped; dictators' armies marched.

'*I've come for my music, Dad*'. Myer stood uneasily
in the unlit hall. '*I've got a job – in Mary's Café,
the Arcade, Corporation Street… playing with band
every afternoon. You know, teatime swishy stuff.*'
Grandpa – (it's anecdotal) – walked upstairs backwards,
carved buttons like piano keys, all black. The doctor came.

Leaving Mozart, Mendelssohn, for Porter and Novello,
no Grand Hotel, pier-end orchestra or failing theatre,
would do without a girl, a horse, a race each afternoon.
A trail of missed engagements, broken dates, arthritis.
The Playhouse closed that week for overdue repairs.
A seizure in his sitting room, the curtains drawn.

Writing To Rita, 1944

I wrote to Rita Hayworth once.
It was that short-trousered time
of ration books and gas masks
in cardboard boxes; and fear,
kept distanced by balloons,
ears twisting on faery wires
above the city, nightwise
sleeping on Bakerloo and District
Lines that took us swiftly home
after seeing Rita Hayworth.

'Dear Rita, I loved that film –
you were super in the part
of Gilda – I'd like a photo'
to pin on the bedroom wall
where gas street lights once
threw shapes I could imagine
from *The Hotspur*'s weekly heroes.
Your golden halo will be hung,
ascending, above Mum's purple lino.

The V1's engine cuts. Wait.
A pubertal heartbeat thurrumps
isthisit isthisit isthisit isthis...
And Chatsworth Road wakes in dawn
overtures of sweeping glass ripped
from streets across the railway line.
Survival is time regained; and painful
to ink out that longing, shifting,
deep aching in the loins
for hips swathed in silk

and lips lustier than any
in the road. Oh Rita, Rita,
nothing could be sweeter
than your picture on the wall.
'Miss Rita Hayworth, Hollywood, USA'
Postman, please send my letter over
convoy-dotted seas to the land
of Hershey Bars, fake mansions, pools of blue,
those crowded, smoky, sexy dives with you.

More glass music. Houses into holes.
Such long, long nights under beds
or hunkered down on basement coals.
Balloons swing idle in August air;
my guts untethered, churn, prepare
the Forties' cocktail – Fear With Lust.
Will the postman ever come? He must.
A.m. – on the 'WELCOME' mat one shiny card.
On her bed, my goddess, golden, haloed, sprawled.

'With fondest love – Rita'. Postmarked USA.

Returning to FR Leavis

(i.m. Jim Prowse)

We went to Leavis' lectures
once or twice perhaps.
Mill Street – two lanes down
from King's.

Literature in February frost
and college scarves, bikes
jammed in the sheds.
We sought enlightenment.

I can't recall a word he said
except that DH Lawrence
was the one and true.
I remember the open shirt.

The lapels wide on his jacket
and most, the commanding head;
he has his biography now.
And you?

Nothing Should Interrupt...

Nothing should interrupt the writing
of a poem except a window glance.
My little closed-off world outside,
waves footling loose as smoke
on the stretched mask of the lake.
My neighbour's savage prunings
of ancient apple, pear, Victoria plum,
in February fire, are smoke in waves

drifting past this glass, that birch,
and bird cherry, crowded hawthorn,
ready to be layered for a second life.
So Rilke – sitting alone – writes
'*Siehe; die Baume sind; die Hauser,*
die wir bewohnen, bestehn noch. Wir nur...' *
preferring on his daughter's wedding day
his window to church pew, his verse to her.

Cut to family guest, who noticed absence
tut-tutted, told. Or, was it rumour
about this man; poems counting more
than love, selfish but true? Yet, he saw,
as I do here, the marvel of budding trees,
treeness, standing strong, true as houses do.
And me? Temporary, moving, being moved.
smoke in waves '*Austausch... luftiger.*' **

* 'Look, trees do exist; the houses that we live in still stand. We alone...'
** 'fugitive... as the wind'. RM Rilke (1875-1925) from the Second Duino Elegy.

Boat Song At Loweswater

Unshackled from post and padlock
the boat slides to water, smooth as eel.
Sun blinks on the brass rowlocks' cup,
on two score of dull bronze nails Ulysses
would have known of and approved.

Sun blinks, on, off, through umbrellas
of ash, skeletons of nascent leaf,
on gear oarsmen, galley slaves,
look-outs, sea-dogs have used since
Homer recalled a wine-dark sea.

Winter quarters, caves, sheds by yards,
spawn *verd de Grece*; tainted air
spots familiar metal, as age scars
skin. Short term, temporary, the greeny dew
is no defect. It's just the way things are.

Born in darkness, a curse of metal
goes, the bow, bead-wet, sharp, shining,
cleaves the lake's skin, pulls it back.
We're opening curtains in a huge room.
Walls, ceiling, bright mirror are the fells,

the boat, angle of the meeting-place,
matrix for larch, rock and birdsong,
infinite light, and us together to celebrate.
We've pushed out the boat. Watch it ride.
Be our swan, our coracle, our leaky caravel

with no coast in sight, our waiting ship of death?
Pushing out the boat is what we have to do.
Stow oars, rudder, drift, drift, along the shore,
speechless in the sacrament of what we see.
Another boatman will find a post to moor.

Second-Hand Silence

They doused seven candles to touch darkness
inside and out, stood overcoated, the family group,
as if a local photographer with lens and hood
waited by some garden gate for the final snap.

Waiting were lorries, murmur of engines
exhaling slow drifts of smoke in side streets,
and more rebuffs to silence, the voices;
children's voices, shrill, quickly subdued,
asking why candlelabra lay under snowdrops
beside plate, sports cups, the Great War sword,
Iron Cross for bravery at the Front, why Hansi
had been put down, cats left to stray, hunting
for rats; and neighbours drew curtains, argued,
later picked locked doors, self-help to what
couldn't be panicked into one case per person
and bedding rolls; the youngest bemused
how at midnight mother wears best dress, fur tippet,
muff, father a favourite suit, with newish fedora.

So where's the microphone to overhear slam
of tail-boards, howl of disowned animals, footfall,
lorries in side streets, the usual cool south wind
which, another night, fought to bend and break
silver birches on the lakeshore, disturb water
near a villa fierce with light, as plans were made
between cigars, the best cognac, the finest glass.

No, none of this was filmed by newsmen, caught
in the scratchy far-offness of shellac discs and yet,
forever second-hand, absent, users of what isn't ours,
obsessed, puzzled, readers, students of memorials,
we'll never see what they saw, nor have to still
voices of children, faced with unknowing,
instead wrestle with the sense of this:

'*I would like to write and remain silent.*'*

* Janos Pilinszky (1921-1981)

Note: The villa is Am Grossen on Wannsee outside Berlin, where on 30th January 1942, a group of Nazi leaders and civil servants decided on the 'Final Solution'.

Two Men In A Boat

He holds the oars as if these might be helping hands
and as he's told, 'dip them, dip them in the lake',
those eyes I've watched a lifetime say 'I don't understand'.
This boat's a clinkered spinning top; currents take

command. Water swirls. A newly varnished bow is scraping
shadowed stones. He reaches out to connect, to align our touch.
I know this isn't love but need. That I've been waiting
forty years for sentences, words. Dear God, can it be too much

for unbelievers to ask for signs? Grab oars, push off the beach.
Marsh marigolds sink yellow into grass. Early pipistrelles weave
skaters lines in air. He can't marvel at flight's surprise, nor reach
places of stored delight; heather, sunshot, fading, a raddled sleeve

on Grasmoor's flanks, Red Pike, Low Fell, High Stile.
We live in silence, to face each other. A trout is rising
at the stern. 'Trout'. 'Bbrout'. Echoing me, his mouth will
hurt with emptiness. One tongue slowly learns to sing.

Agua At Capilliera

Today a scarf of sky tightened over the sea.
It will not yield to prayer nor imprecation.
Here in the high valley, short – changed on spring,
snared under cloud fat as puffed eiderdown,
I ask, why heat and sun and light are wasted
on oiled beaches, striped umbrellas of Malaga,
the coast road's crumpled cars, but refused
the old Moor's stacked terrace across the gorge
beyond the fig tree (waiting to have its shadow
etched on the garden wall of Casa La Fragua),
and won't unclasp for summer the snow necklace
of the Sierra, make those chill pearls water.

Not A Tale From Ovid

Polymathus, demi-god, sometime adjutant to Vulcan,
stretched two withered arms high and yawned.
Took off his dirty nightcap, belched like Bacchus
did at lunchtime each fine blue Naples day, and
belly swollen farted hard and long. *'It's time'*,
he said, *'the heat is in my rocky loins'*. The great
bed buckled, its iron plates shaking as he rose
in the cavern bedroom. The walls sundered, fell

just when the whore, Clytoris (her silken thighs much
praised by Pliny in letters* to his son) pouted
to a golden mirror,with lipstick newly brought
from Leptis Magna by a commander of the Tenth,
and stroked the mouth old senators adored.
Then Earth moved for real; *'it's real'* she cried,
running at the door and reached it. The latch
broke in her hand. Her dog – he'd seen plenty –

twenty years of lust, liaisons, libations, –
friendly Titus Critus, the diamonds in his ears
were often admired at parties, barked only once.
Next door in the Street of Oranges, in the marble
swimming pool with frescoes of copulating swans
water tilted ninety degrees, the floor went
dry and buttocky bathers, grabbing towels, crawled
across the tiles and died. It was dark at noon

that day, pumice floated in the mist, ashy – thin,
flaky as leper's skin, on the torn and scarlet
surface of the bay. There Polymathus saw
himself, inverted, cone-shaped, belching,
farting fire. Buttoning a coat of grit, he slept.

Epistolae Plinius. Volume 3, pp 79-80, D Leier, Tauschnitz (ed), Berlin, 1893.

The Second Page Of A Journal Of A Tour In Asia Minor – Manly Virtues

When Alexander came to Goçek,
whatever its name, in 333,
he demanded wine and meat
for fifteen thousand men,
women for idle evenings,
hay for horses from the lush
pastures old Homer marketed
as green and broad and rich.
The onward slog to Issus,
to snare Darius, to grab an empire
would be, – he scratched his head
that God-like morning – a slog.
Mountain, forest, passes, river –
angry Xanthus frothed in spate –
at sixteen hundred stadia distant
stood Termessos, rock-fast, daunting,
walled, *'impregnable'* know-alls said.
He'd sent the two top scouts.
Their nose for danger highly regarded,
Karpos and Meliparos, could run
with desert wolves, climb like goats,
tease out routes, find hidden trails.
'King' – this was familiar speech,
comradely Macedonians
didn't stand on ceremony.
'King'… 'it's really well defended,
a stonker', Karpos added, *'but*
you could take it in the night.
A fight, of course, but we will win.

Yes – and, King, the temples ooze
with gold'. That did it. No mistake.
There were no longer hours
or days to enjoy this place.
this good place, the lazy sea,
the pinewood scents,
women, broad-hipped and beautiful,
wine that slapped the throat,
the peppered roasted meats.
The army packed its tents,
untethered, reluctantly,
the hardly rested horses,
moved on. Alexander, ever
at the head, dust rising, talks
of going home next year.

Prayer Book

Hidden, shelf-bound, between God and Ghetto,
between Plock lanes and Wilno's yards.
between *haggadah* and *halakah*,
between myths, facts, and second-order history.

Opened on Sabbath, once handled by the dead,
consulted for reference, illustration,
inherited with Dresden china, Berlin plaques,
a portfolio of shares in blue-chip companies

which dealt in aircraft, high explosive, gas.
If it's dropped, pick it up, bestow a kiss,
gently like a lover, blow off dust.
When torn, rebind, mend the tears.

Forgotten for two uncertain generations.
For ever? That might be better, safer,
wiser, braver, politically correct.
Read it for the hour the dustman calls,

for night, the moment two black policemen kick the door;
for dawn, an unsteady walk down curtained streets;
for morning, trucks waiting at sunlit platforms;
for dear neighbours, who look the other way.

Wonder, holding it, who owned you,
what cut of suit, colour of dress, line of hem?
New rich, endowed in mink; or poorer,
in hand-me-downs from bargain stores?

Father in a bowler hat and *tallus*,
uncles, aunts in cotton prints.
Opened, page 321 is free
fall in air. *Kaddish*; parents.

Notes:
Haggadah – part of the *Talmud* (the book of civil and religious obedience) recited at Passover.
Halakah – the legal element in the Talmud.
Tallus – prayer shawl.
Kaddish – prayer for the dead since the time of the Crusades.

Diary Note

On Golden Lane, rain-greased, cobbled, sloping,
wind builds untidy heaps from sweet wrappers,
autumn leaves, last week's *Literani listy*.
Visitors fled perplexed to tourist buses.
Your house, tiny as a beetle's back, stands
strangely quiet. Books – 'For Sale' – lined up
in the window like Havel's toy soldiers
(without the chic of slick blue trousers).
Black overcoated, a pale, unhappy face,
your photograph stares out, naked,
yet there's something just a little jaunty
in the hat. Was it that day you'd settled
on good terms a claim about a factory
making bearings, gun sights, ladies' trusses,
then regretted – for several hours – writing
in the octavo notebook you told Max Brod
to burn – *'there is hope but not for us'*.

Note: *Literani listy* – the Prague journal in which Franz Kafka (1883-1924) published
many of his stories.

Found Poem – Israel Type

You are not authorized
to view this page.
You might not have permission
to view this directory or page
using credentials you supplied.

If you believe you should be
able to view this direct-
ory or page, please try to
contact the Web site by
using any e-mail address
phone number that may
be listed on the www.
haaretz.com home page.
You can click Search to
look for information
on the Internet.

I can?

HTTP Error 403 -
Forbidden
Forbidden
Forbidden
Forbidden
Forbidden
Forbidden
Forbidden

Three Notes From Iceland

1. Poets

Jonas Halmgrimsson
Mathias Johnannson
Halgrimmur Peturson
Tomas Gudmunsson
Stephan Stephansson
And so on sson.

2. Icelandic Horses

This is the warmest North
next the Pole.
This emptiest of great skies
might have scared Pascal
but not the small horses
whose smell we missed last night.
Soft muzzles, lank manes,
nosing grass, browsing untethered,
heads down,
readers, books, sagas.

3. Thingvellir

Winds bonsai willows,
small, feathery, soft, lost
in the plain of Thingvellir.
Weak green blossoms
struggle on lava fields.
Earth's crockery breaks
behind a hill. Walking,
we strain for rough
voice of settlers
arguing in the Althing,
crowded booths,
stink of dung.

Four Notes From Ireland

1. Burren Flowers
(after Michael Longley)

Where are you from –
Ancient glacier, cleared forest?
This year it seemed an offering
for us in gryke and summer crevice
clint scooped hollows an inch of earth
grassy hummocks puddled limestone
everywhere the Early Purple Orchid
and shy here-I-am Spring Blue Gentian
Mountain Avens Bloody Cranesbill
Rockrose Dropwort (or Fillyfundillaun –
good for sickness of the kidneys)
how we moved in colour on fertile rock
ripe inviting as Sheila-na-Gigg
love-goddess parting her eroded vulva
above the church doorway of Kilnaboy.

2. Burren Walls

The stones conspire in uprightness
as if the builders had dealt
out cards not limestone slabs
such jagged raggedy ranks
craggy hearts rough diamonds
clubs spades some other crazy
shape so lightly tip-touching
hugging against tomorrow's fall
embracing over portholes
where wind's an Irish whistle
and eyes take on the rain.

3. Global Warning

Five past midnight
five past midnight
said the climatologist
swans tread water on Inchiquin.

4. Wild Swans At Coole
(after WB Yeats)

Swans are part of this place.
Dimly white and islanded
the far-off four won't approach.
And the other nine-and-forty six
great winged siblings?
Gone with the great house?

Blakeney Point With Or Without Bottles

It's a crescent moon, this marsh river,
with broken skiffs and posher boats
kebabed on sleek mud flats waiting
tidal lift – off which is now as sea
whisks in from Holland, or just over there
beyond the scrub, dune hills, grass
sporting this way and that like wayward
children flying haphazardly with the wind.
And where, my darling, is the bottle
you launched last year in Ecuador
with a precious message *'I love you'*.

Here, across the creek – water gathers pace,
gathers pace – is lovely emptiness. Faint,
and weak the closing sun musters a glitter
of possibility, looks downwind this butt-end
of afternoons. We'd seen huge shred fields,
felt warm air clotted in storms of chaff
from monster combines roaring, cutting,
grinding, – *'give us this day our daily bread'*.

At Blakeney the blonde paymaster shouts
'it's pay up time' – signs us off the clipboard
into rejigged lifeboats which ferry punters
in painted toenails and Primark flipflops
to ooh agh the Blakeney seals at ease before
a swish of oars and folk memory of pain
sends them a-slither-wither into the safe hold
of the North Sea that's whisking in from Holland
as it's always done, always done, always done,
with or without bottles and messages of love.

Vol de Nuit

(for Hetty)

Sharing joy, the look on your face,
in the pouch of your eye,
you said, quietly, weighing,
trapped in a muslin bag,
the tiniest bundle in the world
'four grammes, flesh and fur'
then parted its wings in a gentle fan.
Snarling pointy teeth, our bat launched
from the table, our angry hurdler
facing a last jump, flew to the sink.
Fifty seconds of excited flutter
to a grand circle of applause
refugee, asylum seeker, soprano pipistrelle
saved from a Woolworth's bin.
He left, looping with panache
into night, the windows casements
opening magically on air and tree
and unsuspecting midges
weaving the last wild waltz.

Coda

By the old water butt
The red squirrel watches.
A hose drips.